FORMING

—— THE ——

FORMLESS

Accessing and Elevating Your Spirit and Soul

JASON SHURKA

PAGE PUBLISHING, INC.
Conneaut Lake, PA

First originally published by Page Publishing 2019

jasonshurka.com

ISBN 978-1-64628-511-2 (pbk)
ISBN 978-1-66240-093-3 (hc)
ISBN 978-1-64628-512-9 (digital)

Printed in the United States of America

DEDICATION

I would like to humbly dedicate this book to every reader who attracted it into their lives. You picked up this book for a reason. This reason may not be apparent right away, but I assure you that it was no accident. If you are reading this book, it means that you are ready to receive the information that is contained herein and dive deep within your soul. May this book be the beginning of a new awareness and consciousness about your life, journey, and destiny. I wish each and every one of you a journey of elevation filled with Light, Peace, and Love.

CONTENTS

ACKNOWLEDGMENTS

First and foremost, I would like to thank and honor the Universe for giving me the love and motivation to write this book. I am thankful for all the experiences its infinite realm of power has given me. Thank you for all the information I was allowed to access and for giving me the opportunity to share it with the rest of the world.

To my incredible parents, Manny and Marcy, thank you for guiding me and supporting me throughout my life. You have provided me with incredible tools to assist me in elevating my soul. You have given me the opportunity to travel the world and experience life through a multitude of lenses, each yielding a different perspective. The belief each of you have in me has propelled me beyond the stars. Thank you for showing me unconditional love and instilling Light, Peace, and Love within my soul.

To my beloved sister, Ashley, I am grateful for the unconditional connection we have for one another and for the growth you have led me to experience. We may be very different, but that difference is what has contributed to my growth by challenging my mind time after time. You have led me to think and experience from different lenses that transcend my own. The experiences that we have shared together have led me to understand some of the most valuable lessons I hold dear to me. Thank you for your support and always being by my side. I love you.

To my dear soul friend, Talia Havakook, words cannot express the amount of gratitude I feel in every fiber of my being for allowing us to cross paths in life. The beauty of who you are is that your perfection in everything you do is absolutely effortless. You have taught me what unconditional Love truly is as it is the only kind of love that exists within you. Thank you for being a bright Light in my life. Thank you for being by my side through my hardships. Your soul is a natural projector that illuminates every single being that it comes in contact with. Thank you, my soul friend, for so naturally being pure. I love you.

To my dear friend, Damien Wynne, thank you for all the hours you have invested in me. You have helped me expand and elevate beyond what words can describe. I am appreciative of all the power you have allowed me to reveal from within myself. I thank the universe every day for allowing us to cross paths. May you progress on your incredible path of healing humanity.

To my true friends who have helped me along the way—Esther Zernitsky, Orna Ben Omri, Tamar Reich, Anton Livshin, Michael Golpanian, Malka Krieger, Yaniv

Ariel, Matthew Terbancea, Liran Azizian, Romi Lipetz, Lloyd Leary, Benny Carmazi, Nina Shapir, Lee Najman, Blaine Klusky, and Tom Lodi—I am eternally grateful for all of you in my life. Thank you for always being by my side and engaging with me in deep, thought-provoking conversations. You have all been a part of my spiritual growth. Thank you for challenging my mind and being a part of my journey of elevation.

I am grateful for all those whom I have ever come in contact with. No matter the experience we shared together, whether brief or prolonged, I have learned something from every one of you.

You have all been a part of my journey and, therefore, a part of my growth. I am thankful to all of you for providing me with experiences that have brought me to where I am today. You have all made this book possible.

The universe has foundational laws by which it works. We must understand these universal foundations to be able to control manifestation between the formless and the formed. Once these laws have been internalized and understood, controlling our lives will be as simple as flipping a light switch. To attain this level of being, we must first dissolve all illusions and see the universe in its rawest form—the formless realm.

We live in a world of illusion. What we think we see is not always what it seems to be. We have been taught by society to think in conventional terms, such as beginning, end, birth, death, creation, destruction, good, bad, and so on. All these words are used to describe concepts that are not real. They are illusions. These concepts have all stemmed from the lack of understanding of the laws that govern the universe—the foundations. If we do not understand the foundations, the world will forever be an illusion to us. The information that exists within this book is broken up into two parts: "Foundations" and "Illusions." **You must first read and understand the foundations. Only then will you be able to understand the illusions.** The foundations are meant to reveal the universe in its raw form. They will give you the ability to perceive the world from a lens of truth, rather than from one of illusion. Once the foundations are understood, internalized, and digested, the illusions will be apparent. They will be obvious. They will no longer be illusions to you. More importantly, once the foundations are truly understood, you will achieve full control of your life. You will attain a higher level of consciousness. You will be granted access to the formless realm, where all form is created.

Ever since I could remember, I saw things differently, did things differently, and understood things differently than others around me. As a kid, the universe interested me. The stars interested me. Questions that did not have answers were the ones I asked most frequently: "What is God?" "How was the universe created?" "What happens after we die?" I enjoyed conversations regarding the eternal essence of the universe. In elementary school, all my peers were still imaginative, so my thoughts were not yet shaped by social norms. However, as I got older and gained more social experience, I realized the gap between myself and others around me was only getting wider. What interested me did not interest them. I was different. This difference made it seem as if there was something wrong with me. I felt like I didn't belong. So, I did what any other little boy would do. I changed. Or better put, I "adapted." Over the next ten years, I became a master at fitting in. I became so good at this act that I forgot my true self. I lost touch with my connection to the eternal and infinite universe. I did what I felt I had to do to fit in. I became the popular kid in school, the center of attention at all times. Little did everyone know, including me, it was all an act. I was taught to think, feel, and act a certain way by society. I became a product of the domesticated society we live in. Then, in 2011, a series of painful injuries that forever changed my life began.

The story that I am about to share is not one to be pitied, as there is greater hardship in the world. My intention is to show you how **within every hardship, there is an opportunity**. An opportunity to learn. An opportunity to improve. An opportunity to grow! This principle applies to every hardship, no matter how extreme or severe. I am grateful for the hardships I went through because they are what forced me into a state of self-reflection. They made me stop and think about my life. They made me ask myself, "Why me?" They were the catalyst to my growth and have played a big role in making me the person who I am today.

Between the years 2011 and 2015, I had a series of painful injuries. In 2011, I dislocated my shoulder for the first time. Over the next year, the same shoulder dislocated several more times until I was forced to undergo surgery. After a long recovery, I went back to my daily life. One year later, I dislocated my shoulder yet again. After going through an emergency surgery, the doctor informed me that if this ever happened again, I would need a mechanical shoulder. I took this very seriously and was as careful as can be. Three years went by smoothly until one morning I woke up and my shoulder was out of place. It dislocated in my sleep. I realized I had a major problem. The only thing I could think of was the fact that at such a young age, I would need a mechanical shoulder. Anxious and afraid, I returned to my doctor. He informed me of one last but extreme surgery we could try before resorting to a mechanical shoulder. The surgery was a success, but the recovery was no walk in the park.

One year following the surgery, having fully healed, I had the incredible opportunity to go backpacking in Thailand. What started as a dream ended in a nightmare. I fell during a hike one day and scratched my leg pretty badly. One cut, in particular, was more painful than the others, but I didn't think much of it because of how small it was. A few days went by, and the pain only got more intense. Not understanding where the pain was coming from, I took some Advil and went to sleep early only to wake up multiple times throughout the night with extreme pain. I knew that I had to seek immediate help, so I got on the next plane back to New York. It took me twenty-six agonizing hours to get back home—twenty-six hours with the most intense and excruciating pain I had ever experienced. Some of the flight attendants were crying just hearing me yell in my seat. The second I landed in New York, my family picked me up and rushed me to the hospital. It was midnight when I arrived, so the nurse told me I would not be able to see a doctor until the next morning. I didn't know what the problem was, but I knew that it was urgent. It couldn't wait until the next morning! All I could do was scream, and indeed my screaming was what saved my leg and potentially my life.

A surgeon was in the emergency room that same night visiting a friend. On his way out, he heard my screams and asked what was going on. The nurses explained, and he decided, out of the kindness of his heart, to help me—a deed for which I will forever be thankful. I will never forget the words that came out of his mouth. "Jason, I am not a gambler, but if we don't drain your leg right now, you may not have it tomorrow morning." I immediately demanded that he do so.

"But there's a catch," he said. "I can't numb you."

I had no choice. So, he did what he had to do. He stuck a scissor deep in my leg and opened the cut even further to drain it. Enough liquid to fill a soda can poured out of my leg. The pain I experienced that night was beyond any pain imaginable. I was informed that if I had waited just another eight hours until the next morning for a doctor, my left leg would have required amputation. I had a staph infection. I spent the next week, including my birthday, in the hospital. A week full of intense thought, self-reflection, and introspection.

My numerous injuries had one thing in common. They all resulted in me being in isolation for periods of time. Whether I was in a hospital bed or recovering at home, I had no choice but to be in solitude. They all forced me into a position of self-reflection and meditation. It took me time to realize, but the universe was screaming at me to wake up, to stop living my life acting like somebody who I was not, to stop damaging myself physically and emotionally for the sake of "fitting in," to realize the Light and allow it to dissolve the darkness that lived within me. After twenty-three shoulder dislocations, three shoulder surgeries, and coming very close to having my leg amputated, I woke up. And so, my journey began.

During the past couple of years, I have practiced letting go of the illusory self that I pretended to be throughout my previous years and began reconnecting to my true self. I've had times of struggle; however, within each struggle, I found a seed of growth. I've had the fortunate opportunity to indulge in unique experiences. For my twenty-first birthday, I was given the opportunity to take thirty days to myself in solitude in which I chose to go on a thirty-day juice fast to cleanse and elevate my soul. I met incredible people. I read extraordinary books. I indulged in introspection and meditation. And above all, I wrote it all down. I am no more special than any one of you reading this book. No matter what hardships you are going through, whether it be life-threatening or just a small emotional bump on the road, there is always a lesson to learn. **The more difficult the hardship, the more valuable the lesson.**

This book is a consolidation of the lessons I learned over the past few years through the experiences I endured. It is a combination of the realizations and ideas that I wrote down throughout my times of isolation and meditation. The purpose of this book is to open your doors of thought and allow you to realize the infinite wisdom that exists within you and to light up the darkness within you. The intention of this book is to bring a new level of consciousness to the way you perceive and experience your life. In doing so, you will be able to gain complete control of what your past way of thinking told you that you couldn't.

You can, you shall, and you will if you want!

This book is meant to be used as a guide to help you realize what already exists within. It will only shed Light where darkness may reside. It will assist you in revealing and awakening the wisdom and knowledge that you already possess. After all, wisdom cannot be taught; it can only be attained through the medium of knowledge and experience if transmuted correctly. **You cannot learn wisdom; you may only reveal it.**

The following ideas and concepts are not meant to give you conclusions and answers about how the universe works. Rather, they are meant to simply open your doors of thought for you to explore further and perceive the world in your own unique way. Take your time and read each sentence carefully. Consider reading some chapters more than once, perhaps even multiple times. Allow your soul to digest the information it is receiving and the wisdom it is revealing. **Where you take it is up to YOU!**

A few years ago, a good friend and I sparked an incredible conversation. Not a long one, but a deep one. The conversation ended with one simple question:

> "Jason, if you could choose one person to emulate, dead or alive, who would it be, and why?"

My answer was simply "Nobody." Not Gandhi. Not Martin Luther King. Not Mother Teresa. No one. Although there is a lot to learn from these great people, following their direct individual paths will result in no change in the world other than what had already been done. Although they all embodied traits that create a "better" basis of being, such as optimism, acceptance, kindness, and unconditional love, the combination and the way these traits are applied are what truly matter. It is what creates originality. Look at it like a Rubik's Cube. It only has twenty-six individual pieces with fifty-four different, visible squares, and yet there are over forty-three quintillion different combinations. Just as we know every side to a Rubik's Cube, we also know every trait that exists: kindness, compassion, and acceptance, to name a few. I am not proposing that there are traits that we have not discovered yet. On the contrary, I believe we have discovered every trait and every quality. **We know all our sides. However, we do not know all our combinations.**

The problem is that we are working blindly, trying to make sense of a limitless universe with limited measures—the rational mind and **the ego**. However, if we as human beings take it upon ourselves to become more conscious and aware of not only our surroundings but also our inner stillness, the Light will rise, and the darkness will dissipate. The ego will dissolve, and an innate guide will naturally lead the way. This guide is called **intuition**. Once we allow intuition to become our guide, blinded reason that is constrained with the limitations of the mind will disappear. Consciousness, awareness, and presence dissolve these limitations, in turn going beyond the mind. By being conscious, aware, and present at all times, naturally, the people around you will do the same. **The energy you emit is what others receive**. This in turn will naturally create a chain reaction of awareness across all of humanity and bring about a new wave of consciousness. The person I would like to evolve into will consist of traits and qualities that have existed since the beginning of time, however, not by adopting the combination of traits that great people such as Gandhi, Martin Luther King, and Mother Teresa embodied but by making a completely new combination.

This conversation had a major impact on me—one that reinforced my purpose in life: to transmute knowledge and experience into wisdom, spread it to the rest of humanity in order to raise the vibration of our collective consciousness, and dissolve all illusions and give humanity a brand-new lens to perceive the universe. A clean lens. The information that exists in this book is not new. It is simply a different combination of the Rubik's Cube—one that I hope will bring you closer to the Light and thus dissolve any darkness that resides within you.

PART ONE

Foundations

The law of conservation states that energy cannot be created or destroyed. Understanding such a law is the first step to enlightenment. Understanding such a law brings one to the realization that all existence is not bound by any constraints, such as beginning, end, birth, death, creation, destruction, good or bad. These are merely words that lead you into a world of illusion. The only thing that exists is the transformation of the ever-present formless realm. That which is one, whole, eternal, unchanging, limitless, and timeless.

CHAPTER 1

The Formless Realm

**Everything that ever
existed and will ever
exist originated from the
same place. This place
cannot be understood
by the mind. It can only
be felt with the soul.**

The world of physical form is just a small fraction of our universe. The world of physical form is one grand illusion. It is an illusion that has run our thought processes for millennia. It has caused us to believe in limitation. It has tricked us into thinking that we are bound to birth and death. It has deceived us into thinking that we are limited to the constraints of our physical body. It is an illusion that leads to an array of other illusions. Look at anything around you that has taken a physical form: your car, your phone, your couch, your bed, and your home! Before your home took physical form, what was it? Where did it exist? What form did it take? Confused yet? Before it existed as the physical home you live in, it existed as a thought in someone's mind. From the thought came the design. Architects and engineers were hired to put this design on paper. Then contractors, electricians, and plumbers were hired to manifest the drawing into a physical reality. The fact is that this home began as a thought in someone's mind. Anything and everything you created and will ever create first must have originated in your mind as a thought. The question that remains is "Where did that thought originate from?" Where did it exist before it was formed? This place is what I like to call *the formless realm*.

The formless realm is where all form is derived from. This includes anything tangible or intangible, whether it be a thought, an emotion, a book, a house, or a human being. Look at everything around you, and this includes yourself. Trace its history. Try to break it down to find where it originated from. You will find yourself in a bottomless pit. You will find that everything can be traced back to one place: the line between the formed and the formless. The line of the unknown. The reality here is that **everything that exists originated from the same place**. I call this place *the formless realm*.

To try to describe such a concept through the use of words is impossible because of the inherent limitations of language. Limited words cannot describe something of limitless nature. To describe the formless realm through the use of words is the equivalent of attempting to measure the infinite with a ruler. The only words that can bring you close to connecting to such a concept are ones that dissolve all limitation. The formless realm exists absolutely and indefinitely. It is **one indivisible essence that consists of infinite combinations of form**. That which is **one, whole, eternal, unchanging, limitless, and timeless**.

Forming the Formless

To form the formless for practical purposes, one must remember that form always stems from the formless. All form is interconnected through the formless realm. Forgetting this very fact leads to the illusion of separation, limitation, and death of all form and existence. The factor that leads to this illusion is the desire of the ego to know the unknown, to form the formless, and to limit the limitless. It will do whatever it can to ensure its survival within you, even if that means living a life that is guided by illusion.

Giving the formless realm a name would be doing exactly what we did with words such as beginning, end, birth, death, creation, destruction, good, and bad. It would be acting through the ego. To give form a label and identity is to limit the nature of a limitless and eternal realm. For practical purposes, this is okay to do. However, we tend to forget the formless realm and thus enslave our minds to the illusion of limited form. You must always remember that all form stems from the formless realm. Once form has emerged from the formless, it cannot be destroyed. It cannot endure death. It can only transform. **Death and destruction only exist when the ego is in control.** Once the ego is dissolved, death and destruction become illusory words to describe transformation. **Once the ego is dissolved, beginning, end, birth, death,**

creation, destruction, good, and bad will all be understood as different phases of the same cycle. That which is one, whole, eternal, unchanging, limitless, and timeless. That which all form is derived from—the formless realm.

CHAPTER 2

The Ego

**The ultimate aim of the ego is not
to see something, but to be something.
Become it and you will fall.
Dissolve it and you will rise.**

—Muhammad Iqbal

When I refer to the ego, I am referring to that little part of you that always wants to give reason to the world around you—the part that tries to figure out what you did wrong this week when something unpleasant happens to you, the part of you that always wants to understand the unknown and thus creates stories for temporary closure, the part of you that attaches itself to a viewpoint and deems anyone that disagrees with that viewpoint to be wrong, the part of you that does not like the idea of the formless because the formless has limitless attributes that the ego cannot understand and therefore refutes. It is the part of you that likes using the words *beginning*, *end*, *birth*, *death*, *creation*, *destruction*, *good*, and *bad* because limitation exists within those words, and **a limited mind can only understand something of limited nature**. Your ego is the part of you that tries to be something instead of trying to see something and thus creates limitation. It likes pretending to know the unknown, to limit the limitless, and to form the formless. The ego loves limitation. It is the source of all fear and illusion.

You Are Not Your Thoughts

You have been domesticated by conventional society. We all have. You have been trained to identify with your thoughts for the sake of closure with the unknown—the unknowable and the incomprehensible. **To "know" means to limit all other possibilities.** The mind is a great servant but a terrible master. Identifying with such a great tool renders you unable to use the tool correctly. You must use *it*. Do not let *it* use you!

You are not your thoughts. Your thoughts are simply cars passing by as you watch them from the side of the road. You are the bystander watching the cars pass. To think you are your thoughts is to stand in the middle of the road. You will surely get hit. Thinking you are your thoughts is to derive your sense of self from temporary forms that are subject to change. **If you derive your sense of self from anything subject to change, sooner or later, when that change occurs, your foundation will crumble, and you will be lost in a repetitive cycle of dissatisfaction.** This is what the ego does. The ego feels the constant need to attach itself and identify with thoughts and ideas for the sake of closure. By identifying with a thought or an idea, you have entered a world of limitation—one where an open mind does not exist and, therefore, growth is stagnant. What happens if your thought is challenged? If someone disagrees with the viewpoint from which you derived your sense of self, you will naturally be in a position of defense, since the challenge of that very viewpoint threatens the foundation of who you are—your sense of self. Sooner or later, your sense of self will be lost, and the cycle continues.

The Einstein Effect

For hundreds of years, humanity was under the impression that time was absolute. This idea was held as a law proposed by Isaac Newton. For hundreds of years, this idea was taught in universities across the globe. Professors around the world spent their entire careers teaching that time is absolute to thousands of student's year after year. Albert Einstein was the first to openly challenge this idea. He received a lot of backlash from his professors for this. He was thrown out of his classes and almost expelled from school for being such a nuisance to the professors and the beliefs that they identified with. Instead of entertaining his ideas as a possibility, their egos put his ideas down because they felt threatened. Einstein was challenging the beliefs that they built their careers along with their identities on.

Just imagine what would have happened if Einstein proved that time was indeed not absolute. This would mean that everything that had been researched and studied for the past couple hundred years would have been wrong. More importantly, because many people allowed for this idea to become a part of their identity, proving it wrong would mean to dissolve their foundation upon which they built their sense of self. Well, that is exactly what happened. In 1905, Albert Einstein published his theory of special relativity that has changed the world forever. He proved that time was indeed relative, and not absolute, thus shaking the foundations of what physics was built on. The establishment did not want to accept that one of their foundational beliefs was wrong.

The ego feeds on fear and can be very destructive. Just imagine how much further we could have progressed if we no longer let it run our lives. We have become significantly more technologically advanced ever since the theory of relativity has come to light. The one thing that delayed such progression was the ego.

So, how do we prevent this from occurring in the future? Luckily, the answer is very simple. We stop making beliefs a part of our identity. If this was done during Einstein's time, there would have been no resistance, and rapid growth would have occurred. An open mind would have led to intense progress for humanity. Einstein wouldn't have had to journey untouched waters alone. Rather, he would have had the help of many other great minds and progressed much further than he did in his life, thus greatly benefiting humanity.

Dissolving the Ego

When the ego runs your life, identification with thought occurs. Instead of watching the cars pass as a bystander on the side of the road, you are jumping in the middle of the road and stopping the flow of traffic. Think of it as an eternal traffic jam. This traffic jam leads you on a growthless path of stagnation. This is limitation in its purest form. You become stagnant. Growth becomes a pastime.

Change is no longer a part of your life. This, too, is an illusion that you live by when the ego runs your life. The ego lives by illusion. It feeds on fear. Dissolve the fear, and you will dissolve the ego. To do so, **you must not resist the unknown**. You must stop trying to know the unknown. **Acceptance is the Light that transforms darkness**. Realizing that you are not your thoughts takes you out of the repetitive cycle of illusion and fear caused by the ego.

To dissolve the ego simply means to witness your thoughts flush through you with no need to attach and identify with them. It means to accept the unknown with no need to comprehend it. Others can disagree with your viewpoints, thoughts, and ideas. This is okay because your viewpoint is no longer a part of you. Disagreement is no longer a threat to your foundation. When the ego is dissolved, you will be able to converse and think with no attachment to any viewpoint. When the ego is dissolved, you will lead a life of limitless growth and possibilities.

CHAPTER 3

The Language of Energy

**If you want to find the
secrets of the universe,
think in terms of energy,
frequency, and vibration.**

—Nikola Tesla

God, divine intervention, infinite universe, consciousness—these are just a few words of many that can all be broken down to one common denominator: energy. Energy is everything. It is the basis of the universe. It is what anything tangible or intangible can be broken down to. You cannot know what energy truly is because it stems from the incomprehensible formless realm. Trying to do so would just be the ego trying to know the unknown and limit the limitless. Remember, **to "know" means to limit**

all other possibilities. However, it is possible to understand how this mysterious and eternal essence we call *energy* works. **Learning the language of energy will teach you how to think in terms of energy, frequency, and vibration, in turn granting you access to the formless realm.**

Understanding and Harnessing Energy

To be able to think in terms of energy, you don't have to understand what energy is. You only have to understand how it works. This path of thought is what led us to become experts in electricity. We don't understand what electricity truly is, but we do understand how it works.

Electricity is a form of energy like everything else in the universe. It can continuously be broken down into different forms, but eventually, you will reach the line where you can no longer break it down—the line between the formed and the formless or the line of the unknown. You cannot understand what electricity truly is because it, too, stems from the formless realm, a limitless and incomprehensible source. To know how it works, however, is most definitely possible. We have mastered our understanding of the laws of electricity so well that we can light up an entire stadium with the flip of a switch, and we can light up our cities around the world. We have conquered it. We have taken control. Electricity now serves us.

Understanding the language of energy will replace hope and luck with power and control of the world around you. It will change the way you live your life for the better. It will allow you to dissolve illusions and replace them with truths. It will allow you to aim with precision instead of shooting aimlessly. Understanding the language of energy will allow you to be in complete control of what is formed from the formless, thus allowing you to live a life of limitless potential. If you can understand the language of energy just as we understand electricity, your wish will become your command. The good news is, you can. And once you do, the universe will serve you.

Vibration Rules All

All beings communicate through the medium of vibration. Good vibes and bad vibes—these are all vibrations. **Vibration is the universal language** that is responsible for the interconnectivity of all existence. The deer naturally keeps its distance from the lion because it can feel the vibrations that scream danger. The rabbit keeps its distance from the fox for the same reason. Just as animals can communicate through vibrations, we humans are no different. We, too, have the ability to communicate through this universal language. If we were taught to be sensitive and connect to vibration, we would no longer find ourselves in situations that we do not want to be in. **We must learn to become sensitive to the vibrations that exist around us and within us.** To do so, you must learn how to think in terms of energy, frequency, and vibration.

So, how does energy actually work? The formless realm consists of an infinite spectrum of frequencies. All energy exists in the form of vibrational frequency. Everything is vibration. Thought is vibration. Emotion is vibration. Color is vibration. Matter is vibration. What differentiates one form from another is the speed by which each form is vibrating. This vibrational speed is called *frequency*. Some forms exist at a higher frequency while others exist at a lower frequency, but all forms exist at a specific frequency. Many people have been talking about the law of attraction for years. Some believe it. Some don't. However, there is nothing to believe or not to believe. **It is simply the law of vibration. It is a fact of energy.** The law of attraction states that positive or negative thoughts attract positive or negative experiences. In other words, "like attracts like." To understand how this works, you must think in terms of energy, frequency, and vibration. Being able to do so is the master key to living an egoless, limitless, and boundless life.

Do you ever listen to the radio? Whether you listen to AM or FM, have you ever asked yourself what "AM" and "FM" are? The radio works on frequency. The difference between AM and FM is simply how the frequency is being modulated. Regardless, both AM and FM radios work on frequency, which means they both work by the same principles and laws. If you want to listen to the news, you might tune to a specific AM channel, whether it be 1010 AM or 770 AM. If you want to listen to music, you might tune to a specific FM channel, whether it be 104.3 FM or 97.1 FM. You get the idea. The point is that each channel chooses a frequency on which to host their radio shows. By tuning to that frequency, you have gained access to the show and can, therefore, either listen to the news or sing along to the music.

These basic principles of how frequencies work apply to all frequencies in the universe. This includes emotions and thoughts. Love is a frequency. Depression is a frequency. Happiness is a frequency. You can look at these emotions as channels that exist just like 1010 AM or 97.1 FM. **Your mind is the tuner that chooses what frequency it would like to "listen to" through the medium of thought.** If you think depressed thoughts, you are tuning to the radio station of depression and therefore experiencing your life through that lens. However, if you tune your thoughts to happiness, you will experience your life through the lens of happiness and, therefore, perceive the world around you accordingly. **Perspective is subjective. It is dictated by the frequency of thought you choose to tune your mind to.** You are in complete control of what channel you would like to tune into. Now that you are aware of the power of your thoughts, think consciously, and tune away.

Perceiving the world on the energetic level will allow you to gain full control of your life and live in a balanced and blissful state of mind that will open the portals to the deepest and truest levels of life. That which is one, whole, eternal, unchanging, limitless, and timeless—the formless realm. **Thinking in the language of energy will lead you to an intuitive understanding of**

the world around you. By doing so, you will intuitively lead a healthy life both physically and emotionally. The secrets of the universe will no longer be secrets. If only there was a way to be able to see frequency and energy without using expensive scientific machines. Well, lucky for us, there is! The translator of frequency exists around you at all times. Its name is *color*.

Color Speaks

Color is your friend. It is your translator. Have you ever looked at a rainbow? The colors follow a specific order and never deviate from that specific order: red, orange, yellow, green, blue, indigo, and violet. Have you ever asked yourself why? Because color translates frequency. Color and frequency are the same. **Color is frequency.**

You are most probably confused at this point. Just keep reading, and you will understand.

The colors of the rainbow are a direct reflection of the spectrum of frequency. It is the spectrum of frequency in order from slow to fast! Red, orange, yellow, green, blue, indigo, violet. Red is the slowest frequency. Violet is the fastest. You may be asking yourself, *Why does any of this matter? Who cares that color is frequency, and who cares how slow or fast it vibrates?* Well, since color is translating frequency, it is also translating the language of energy—the language you were born to understand. Your ability to understand its translation will give you direct access to the formless realm. Understanding the translation of frequency through color will teach you how to tune your radio to get to the right station. It will grant you access to the depths of the universe where all form is formed.

Gaining such access will turn you into the creator that forms the formless into whatever form it is that you desire to manifest.

The Translation of Color

The human body is a community of different frequencies. There is a map of the human body that has existed for thousands of years. It breaks the human body down to seven major energy centers called *chakras*. Each chakra is associated with a different part of the body. Each chakra is also associated with a different color based on the frequency that part of your body operates on. **Your body is a map of color.**

This chapter will teach you how to use color to assist you in attaining a higher level of emotional and physical balance. However, you must first understand the map of your colorful body to be able to understand its guidance. This chapter will teach you what each color corresponds to both physically and emotionally. The translation of color will allow you to use color as your guide to help you attain whatever it is that you desire in your life. Once you understand this principle, you will be able to use color to assist you throughout your life and access the depths of the formless realm.

Color affects your emotions and your thoughts. It can even tell you what foods are necessary at a specific point in time to rebalance yourself. Additionally, when I refer to food, I am referring to natural food that has not been created or altered by man. **Food is your medicine, and color is your guide.**

Red vibrates at the same frequency of emotions such as hunger, anger, stress, and aggression. It is the most important chakra to keep balanced because it is the foundation of all your higher chakras. On the physical realm, red corresponds to your hips and specifically your legs, which connect your body to the earth. It is the color that connects you closer to the physical realm rather than the spiritual realm. It is a grounding color. An imbalance of your red chakra can cause bowel disorders, urinary problems, and many other muscular issues associated with the hips and legs. If you are experiencing such issues, simply eat foods that are red: tomatoes, strawberries, and red apples. **By surrounding yourself and consuming the frequencies of earth matter that correlate to red, you, in turn, will inherit that frequency and rebalance your imbalance.**

Orange vibrates at the same frequency of feelings such as creativity, ambition, sexual energy, and addictive behavior. It is a color filled with passion and emotional expression. On the physical realm, orange corresponds to the reproductive organs. If you are experiencing a lack of sexual energy, start surrounding yourself with orange frequencies. Eat carrots and oranges. These foods will surely rebalance your sexual energy to a healthy state.

Yellow vibrates at the same frequency of emotions such as positivity, power, inspiration, and intelligence. On the physical realm, yellow corresponds to the spleen and the stomach. It relates directly to digestion. If you suffer from depression or even poor digestion, start spending more time outside in the yellow sun. Eat a mango. Eat a banana. Eat a pineapple. You will soon see that your depression will dissipate as you inherit healthy forms of the yellow frequency from the natural world.

Green vibrates at the same frequency of feelings such as love, compassion, healing, and giving. On the physical level, green corresponds to your heart and lungs. If you are going through a heartbreak, surround yourself with green. Walk around a luscious garden. Eat a kiwi or a green apple. Embrace and inherit a balanced green frequency.

Blue vibrates at the same frequency of feelings such as communication, truth, and balance. On the physical realm, blue corresponds to your throat and your thyroid. If you experience trouble expressing yourself, spend more time sitting by the ocean. Eat blueberries. Visualize a clear blue sky in your mind's eye, and allow the healthy frequencies of blue to rebalance your system.

Indigo vibrates at the same frequency of feelings such as deep thought, intuition, and sensitivity. On the physical realm, indigo corresponds to the pituitary gland. If you are trying to focus or attain a higher level of intuition, eat indigo foods, such as blackberries or plums. Visualize the color in your mind, and see how it affects you.

Violet vibrates at the same frequency of feeling such as high spiritual attainment and realization of the formless realm. On the physical realm, violet corresponds to the pineal gland. If you are in search of attaining a higher level of spirituality, consume foods, such as beets and figs. Doing so will allow you to inherit the highest frequencies in the spectrum of vibration.

Now that you know what each color translates to, you can use color as your guide, and what better way to do it other than using food? After all, **you are what you eat**! Color is your best teacher. If you are experiencing thyroid issues, eat blueberries. If you are experiencing issues with your breath, eat artichoke or asparagus. If you are suffering from addiction of any sort, eat carrots! If you are experiencing digestive issues, eat a banana! You get the idea. The more you learn about which color corresponds to each part of the body, the more intuitive eating healthy will be. You no longer have to be at the mercy of what one doctor says over another or what one study concludes over another. **Opinions change. Frequencies do not.** All you have to do is pay attention to the colors around you. Use color to your benefit! It talks to you every day. Now that you know its language, all you have to do is LISTEN!

The Law of Conservation

Energy knows no beginning or end, no birth or death, and no creation or destruction. **Transformation is all that exists on the energetic level of the universe.** It may be a difficult concept to understand at first because you are programmed to think in the terms your mind can comprehend—beginning, end, birth, death, creation, destruction, good, and bad. Limited terms. Try to think of something with no beginning or end. A circle. Where does it begin? Where does it end? The answer is nowhere. This is exactly how everything in the universe works. It is difficult to disassociate your mind from the terms that society has instilled within you, but, nevertheless, it is possible.

Let's take a piece of paper to represent this idea. Now in your hand exists a piece of paper and a scissor. With only the use of the scissor, can you make the paper disappear? No matter how many times you want to cut the piece of paper, you will never make it disappear. You may cut it into a million little pieces, but making it disappear is not a possibility. **This is because energy cannot be created or destroyed. It can only be transformed.** This is the law of conservation. Now let's add fire into the equation. Instead of cutting the piece of paper, this time, light it on fire. What happens? *"It disappeared!"* you might think. This is an illusion. It transformed into heat and ash, which are simply other forms of energy. The paper did not disappear. It transformed!

Next time you sit down around a bonfire, focus on what is truly happening in front of you. The energy that we call *fire* is not destroying the wood. It is simply transforming it to heat, ash, and smoke, and the transformation continues. **Fire is not a destructive force. It is a transformational force.** The law of conservation exists all around us at all times. It pertains to absolutely everything. Let your thoughts be guided by the law of conservation. Doing so will help you dissolve illusions that limit your perceived potential in life. Dissolve these illusions, and you return to your true self—a being with no beginning or end, bound by neither birth nor death; a being of limitless potential; a being of limitless power.

The Law of Cause and Effect

Every cause has an effect, and every effect has a cause. Many concepts and words exist in our language today that reflect the direct lack of understanding of the law of cause and effect. Just look at the concept we call *luck*. Luck is a concept created by people who simply lack an understanding of the way the universe works. Luck cannot exist. Because every cause has an effect, **what one calls luck is simply the effect of a cause**. Understanding the cause of the effect we call *luck* will no longer make it an event of chance but an event of choice. **Forming a cause will allow you to predetermine its effect**. Doing so will make shooting aimlessly obsolete.

The root cause of any effect you experience in your life is thought. Thought is the medium that allows each and every effect to manifest itself. **Thought is what guides the formless realm to form itself.** Thought is what stands behind every invention and every structure. The watch you wear on your wrist was first a thought before it was created. The home you live in was first a thought before it was designed and constructed. **Thought forms a cause that will always have an effect.** For example, if you think to yourself that you want to be wealthy and live in a large house, then that might lead you to start your own business. The cause was the thought. The effect was the business. By focusing your thoughts on what you desire, you are naturally formulating a cause that will eventually evolve into an effect, and that effect is determined by the cause. Form the cause to predetermine the effect. **Thought is creative**, and the good news is it is in your absolute control. YOU **are the creator.**

Your external reality is a direct reflection of your thoughts. This is because your **thoughts dictate your perception.** Thought creates the lens by which you perceive the world. Thought is why the poor stay poor and the rich stay rich. It is what separates the content from the depressed. Thought is creative and is, therefore, responsible for creating your reality. You cannot control the circumstances you were born into; however, **you can guide yourself out of any situation you do not want to be in as well as into any situation you do want to be in**.

To consciously guide your thoughts with intention is to gain complete control of the circumstances that manifest in your life. **The answers that will guide you onto the right path of thought exist all around you and within you.** Just look at nature. An apple seed will always produce an apple tree. A tomato seed will always produce a tomato plant. Within the essence of each seed exists an intention to grow into a specific tree or plant. In other words, it has formulated a cause. It has predetermined its effect. In doing so, each seed will effortlessly and consistently grow into what it is intended to manifest. **Every**

tree, plant, or flower is the effect of a cause. This is the law of cause and effect in action. May you learn from nature and formulate a cause through your own intention. May you manifest whatever effect it is that your heart desires.

CHAPTER 4

The Line of Manifestation

**Look deep into
nature, and then
you will understand
everything better.**
—Albert Einstein

Throughout my time living in New York City, I desperately tried to grow fruits and vegetables on the little ledge of the window next to my bed. For two years, I was playing the game of trial and error, trying to grow tomatoes, cucumbers, mint, and an array of different herbs. After a long chain of failures, I finally got the hang of it. My herbs, fruits, and vegetables were flourishing in my little one-bedroom apartment. One morning, I woke up to water the plants, and I realized

something that I had never realized before—
something very apparent and obvious, something beautiful. The mint and tomato plant
were both flourishing out of the **same** pot
and the **same** soil. I saw this happening for
weeks and never thought anything about it
until one day I stared at it for a little longer than usual in quiet contemplation. This
moment of silence led me to a realization.
A very important realization—the line of
manifestation.

The concept behind the line of manifestation may seem confusing at first because it
has to do with the limitless, formless realm.
However, it is much simpler than you may
think. The perfect analogy for understanding the line of manifestation exists all around
you, especially in nature or the natural world.
Just look at soil. Out of soil grows everything:
trees, flowers, fruits, vegetables, and plants.
The list goes on and on. It grows everything.

Within soil exists all potential forms. The seed is what forms the soil into its intended form. Soil represents the formless realm of physical nature. Seeds represent our thoughts that form the formless. The fact that the same soil can give life to both a tomato plant and mint shows that the soil is indeed the formless, and the seed is what guides the formless to form.

To learn from nature is to learn from truth. It cannot misguide you because it stems from truth. A watermelon seed will always become a watermelon plant. A banana seed will always become a banana tree. You will never see a banana seed manifesting an apple tree or a watermelon seed manifesting a blueberry bush. Each seed has its own energetic blueprint to manifest into what it is built to manifest. You must learn from nature. You must focus your thoughts and energy on what you would like to manifest with no doubt and no other result in mind other than what you desire. It will surely manifest. **You must focus the energy behind your thought just as seeds focus their energy to manifest their desired creation**, just as a tomato seed intends to form a tomato plant. Seeds do not make mistakes. Nature does not make mistakes. This is because nature works in perfect harmony, and YOU are a part of nature. You have access to perfection because you are perfection.

The Initial Thought

So, how do you focus your energy to manifest what you desire? Well, you do it all the time. Now you are just going to learn how to guide what you already know how to do into the direction that you desire. The law that energy cannot be created or destroyed shows us that anything that has manifested into physical reality was once in the formless state of energy. Whether it be a car, a house, or a tree—its essence has always existed.

Let's revert to the example of the home. Before it existed as a physical home, it first existed as a thought in someone's mind. From the thought came the design. Architects and engineers were hired to sketch the thought into a physical drawing. From there, contractors, electricians, and plumbers were hired to put the home together and construct it the way it was envisioned.

Did you see what just happened there? A home that began as a thought in someone's mind is now a reality. The thinker formed the formless by focusing the energy behind their thought. The thought was the seed of energy that created the home that manifested into physical reality. **Your thought is what dictates the formless to form.** Your thought is the line of manifestation.

Creating Your Seed

Your thoughts are responsible for manifesting all circumstances into your life. Your job, your relationships, your feelings—everything. The key is to be able to control what circumstances manifest, to be in control of your life. As you already understand, **everything that has ever and will ever happen to you is the effect of a cause** just like any plant, tree, or flower that has ever and will ever grow is the effect of a seed. Your thoughts and intentions are what form those causes. **Just as you plant a specific seed to manifest a specific plant, you must create a specific cause through thought to manifest a specific effect.** Create your seed, plant your seed, and let it flourish.

The first step to creating your seed is to visualize it. To make something real, you must first "realize" it. To realize literally means to make real, and where is the only place you can realize anything? Your mind! Yes. The only way to realize something is with your mind. It is the first step in the process of manifesting absolutely anything. It is the first step to creating your seed. Your mind is the medium between the real and the imaginary. Your mind is the tool that stands between the formed and the formless, and your thought is the tool that allows you to form the formless. Your mind is the ultimate tool. Use it. Do not let it use you! **If you can visualize it, you can manifest it.**

Once you visualize your desire, whether it be a brand-new car or a life filled with love and happiness, the blueprint has been created. The second step to creating your seed is to **focus and believe you can achieve your visualization with no doubt or fear whatsoever.** If any doubt or fear exists within you, your seed will be overtaken with poison and will manifest a poisonous plant. Once your belief is set with no alternative result other than what you are aiming for, you must focus your attention back to your visualization. Think about it. Imagine having what it is that you desire. Act like you already have it. The more you focus on your specific goal, the more energy you are giving it to form. **Energy flows where attention goes**. Visualize, believe, focus, and manifest away.

You must always consciously decide where you want to focus your attention, and always remember that it is your decision. **You are in control.** You are not your thoughts. Your thoughts are simply cars passing by as you stand on the side of the road, observing them as they do so. Start making it a habit to observe your own behavior, to witness your own conformity to society that social norms have instilled within you. Set your intention to improve in every aspect of your life, even in places in which you already excel. **Where**

and how you choose to focus your attention will dictate the quality of your life. It will dictate what manifests into your life, whether it be love, health, and happiness or anger, illness, and depression. Focus on negativity, and depression will manifest. Focus on positivity, and happiness will manifest. Focus on lack, and you will gain nothing. Focus on abundance, and you will gain the world.

CHAPTER 5

The Harmony of Balance

**Happiness is when
what you think, what
you say, and what you
do are in harmony.**
—Dalai Lama

I was walking through the forests of Northern California, and suddenly, out of the corner of my eye, I saw a tree engulfed in flames. Out of curiosity, I approached the tree to see what was happening. I quickly realized that it was the beginning of a forest fire. Scared and afraid, I ran as fast as I could from the flames. I made it back to my car and successfully got out of the danger zone! Safe and sound, I had some time to reflect on what just happened.

The only emotion I could experience was gratitude for getting out of there safely.

A few months later, I felt the need to go see what I thought would be a site of destruction. So, I did. **What I saw was not a site of destruction but a site of new creation.** Since the trees burned, they were no longer present to block the sunlight from reaching the ground. The ground that was nothing but dirt and soil a few months ago was now blooming. Grass, flower, and plants were all beginning to sprout. I quickly understood that **without the fire, the ground below the trees would never have bloomed**! This experience caused me to see the world in an entirely different light. I immediately connected to the balance of the universe. **Within every destruction, there is a new creation. Within every end, there is a new beginning.** This is the harmony of balance.

Balance is an eternal law of the universe. To think of anything without it is not possible. The law of cause and effect shows just this. Every cause has an effect, and every effect has a cause. What goes up must always come down. Every action has a reaction. These are basic phrases that you've heard many times throughout your life, but have you ever really given them any attention or thought? Balance is the fuel behind the perfect order of the universe. Balance is what is responsible for all progression and growth. Balance takes away the need to label something positive or negative. It takes away the habit of referring to things as *good* and *bad*. Positive and negative do not exist. Good and bad do not exist. There is no such thing as too much or too little. Everything you need, you have. **Balance is all there is. Balance is harmony.** This is the perfect order of the universe.

Yin and Yang

Light cannot exist without darkness. Peace cannot exist without the experience of war. Love cannot exist without hate. Yin cannot exist without yang. I want you to picture a yin-yang symbol in your mind. If you have never seen one, search one online before continuing to read this passage. It's important that you have a clear image of one in your mind.

Now that you see the yin-yang, whether in your mind or on your computer screen, I want you to take a minute and focus on it. Digest it. Absorb it. What would the light be without the dark? What would the dark be without the light? Without the light, the dark would not exist. Without the dark, the light would not exist. We live in a world where we are always trying to have the light without the dark, the good without the bad, and the happy without the sad. Now look back at the yin-yang. Look at the light half. Now, look at the dark half. Getting rid of one or the other is impossible. They only exist relative to one another.

The Poisonous Illusion

Society has taught us to think that a change in external circumstances will dissolve internal poisons, so we live our lives according to this way of thinking. This is a poisonous illusion that leads us into an endless cycle of unhappiness. The following example is meant to show how this illusion works in our daily lives. On the surface, it may not apply to you. That is okay. The principle is all that matters. Realize this principle, and look where it applies to you in your own life.

You constantly think to yourself, "I am miserable because I can't pay my bills," and this leads to worry and anxiety. "I don't have enough money," you tell yourself. Then you continue to think that if you had more money, you would truly feel great. You think to yourself that if you had more light, the darkness would disappear or would at least get smaller, your bills would be paid on time, your worries would be gone, and your anxiety would cease. So, some time passes, and you attain the level of wealth that you told yourself would make you happy and worriless. Your bills are paid. You can afford luxurious vacations and getaways. You live in a luxurious mansion. You can live the life that you told yourself would make you happy—the life that you told yourself would dissolve all your worries and anxiety.

Some time goes by, and you soon realize that the problems you once had when you had less wealth are now manifesting in different forms. Your worry still exists, just in a different form. Your anxiety still exists; only you are now anxious about different things. You come to see that **your internal emotional poisons, such as worry and anxiety, cannot be dissolved through external means**. To think that the change of your external circumstance will help you attain internal bliss and balance is an illusion. So long as you allow emotional poisons to reside within you, such as worry and anxiety, your thoughts will stem from poisonous seeds, and therefore, your reality will be poisoned as well. **Balance your internal reality, and your external reality will follow.**

Dissolving the Poison

Imagine a tall thick tree. This tree has hundreds of branches and thousands of leaves. It is a beautiful tree! Only there is one problem. The root of the tree is filled with poison. From the root, this poison spreads to the tree trunk and into each and every one of its beautiful branches. Your goal is to keep the tree alive. In order to do so, your first thought is to cut off all of its branches. So that is exactly what you do. Some time passes and the branches grow back, only this time they are different branches. But you realize that the branches are still filled with poison. Why? Because the poison was coming from the foundation of the tree—the root. You endlessly try cutting off the branches only to realize that the poison is not disappearing. New branches are growing, but they are still filled with the poison from the tree's root. You realize that every time you cut the branches, all you are left with is a different set of poisoned and diseased branches when they grow back. **You must tackle the problem by dissolving the poison in the**

root, and only then will the branches no longer be filled with poison and disease. New branches will be able to grow strong and healthy.

The root of the tree represents your thoughts. The branches of the tree represent the circumstances of your life. **If your root is poisoned, your branches will never be healthy.** Any poisonous thought will surely manifest into poisonous circumstances. Thinking that more wealth will dissolve your worry and anxiety is a false and poisonous thought. Attaining more wealth will not dissolve your worry and anxiety. It will only result in the growth of a different branch from the same poisonous root.

Worry and anxiety are emotional poisons. Trying to treat them through external means is like trying to cut off the branch of a tree with a poisonous root and hoping to have a healthy branch grow back. **Changing** your external factors will not dissolve your internal emotions that stem from poisonous thought. It will only make those internal emotional poisons manifest differently. Nevertheless, they will still exist. You will surely get a new set of branches, but they, too, will be poisoned.

The goal is to **clear your root of all poison**. To do so, you must first rid yourself of emotional poisons without giving any regard to your external circumstance. **Resistance is your poison, and acceptance is your antidote.** This is not to be confused with not taking action. If you are in a situation you do not want to be in, then you must first accept the situation. Once you accept the situation, only then can you think clearly about how you would like to change your situation. Do not resist your external circumstances. Doing so will make happiness unattainable. After all,

true bliss is when your inner freedom is not contingent on your external circumstances.

The Power of Acceptance

Visualize your mind as a river. Generally, this river is very clean, but today you decided to dump a bucket of toxic waste, in the form of poisonous thought, into it. You don't like this toxic waste, so you stop the flow of water. This is resistance. **What you resist persists.** This is because when you are resisting, the toxicity can no longer flow out of the river. You essentially just built a dam that now prohibits the toxic water from exiting the river. Acceptance, on the other hand, will allow the toxicity to filter out of the water. It will let the water flow. **Acceptance is your key.**

As yin grows, so does yang. They are always in direct proportion to one another.

However, there is no necessity to see one as good and the other as bad. One is simply light, and the other is simply dark. **Each represents different experiences in life.** Not good or bad, just different halves of the same whole. **No experience is a bad experience because you will always be one experience richer.** Realizing this reality will allow you to transcend the yin and the yang. **To transcend beyond the yin and the yang, acceptance is your key.** Acceptance dissolves the illusion of separation between the good and the bad, the dark and the light. It dissolves the illusion of opposites. Acceptance takes the *and* out of yin and yang. Acceptance makes yin and yang one: yin-yang. Acceptance allows both yin and yang to exist in the same indivisible circle of balance. Accept reality as it is with no inner resistance. **Once you have accepted your circumstances, only then can you act with the intention of changing your cir-**

cumstances from a place where poison is nonexistent. After all, true bliss can only exist in the presence of no resistance. True bliss is pure acceptance, and pure acceptance is true bliss.

One Experience Richer

Take a pen and a piece of paper. Now draw a line representing your emotional and mental growth from your first memory as a child until the present day. Before doing so, give it a few minutes of thought. Think deeply. You will soon realize that this line will indeed show growth; however, before any high point, there is always a low point. Think back to a time of hardship in your life: a breakup, a defeat, the loss of a loved one, or a failure at achieving something. Whatever happened, it was something you experienced. **Within every experience, especially one of hardship, exists**

a seed of growth. Within every failure exists a seed of success. This is the beauty of balance.

The low points are no longer the low points, and the high points are no longer the high points. The low points are simply where you gain new tools and new perspectives, and the high points are where you apply those tools to grow wiser. They only exist in relation to one another. Without one, the other cannot exist.

So, next time you go through a hardship, be grateful. Smile! **You are now one experience richer than you were before.** You've been given an opportunity to grow and evolve into a better, more authentic version of yourself. **The harder the experience, the more potential for growth!** On the other hand, if you don't use your low points to your benefit and if you don't take the tools the universe is giving you, you will enter into an endless cycle of stagnation. If you never realize your tools and use them, you will forever live on the low point. Look at each hardship that comes your way as a test. Fail, and you will have to repeat. Pass, and move on to the next level. **Resist, and you will fail. Accept, and you will pass.**

The next time you feel out of balance, remember that only balance exists. Whether you are sick, tired, or feel you are not happy, **remember that you always have exactly what you need**. Every disease has a cure, even if it has yet to be discovered. Every problem has a solution. Use these basic principles to guide you through life, both emotionally and physically. Realize the beauty of balance that exists around you at all times. See the success within each failure. See the gain within each loss. See the creation within each destruction. See the beginning within each end. See the yin within each yang. They are one and the same. **Look closely, and you will see that balance is all there is, but only if you allow yourself the freedom to see it.** This is the beauty of the universe, the beauty of balance and harmony.

CHAPTER 6

Dive Within

**Knowing yourself is the
beginning of all wisdom.**

—Aristotle

We live in a world where others are constantly trying to find answers through external means. We live in a world where others truly believe that physical scientific instruments will be able to bring us to spiritual truth. We live in a world where others feel that they can gain true happiness and love through the use of material objects. As you may now understand, the world we live in is one grand illusion. Attempting to fix an internal problem through external means is not a possibility. Additionally, **trying to understand the limitless universe through limited means, such**

as physicality, is no different than using a ruler to measure the infinite. It will only lead you into a bottomless pit of dissatisfaction. We are spiritual beings. We are limitless beings. Everything you are searching for exists within you and nowhere else. So, what are you waiting for? Dive within.

Finding Yourself

Look at yourself. You are living in a physical body. You have a heart. You have a head. You have a brain. But if your head is YOUR head and your heart is YOUR heart, then who are YOU? If your body was divided into ten parts and each part was put in a different country, where are YOU? The true question is "What defines YOU?"

YOU are not your money. YOU are not your job. YOU are not your body. YOU are more than the father to your child. YOU are more than the child to your mother. YOU transcend all these things. These are merely identifications that describe your physical existence.

To find yourself, you must not look externally. Searching externally will only lead you to a temporary and illusory conclusion of your sense of self—one that is based on temporary identities, one that is bound to crumble with time. To find yourself, you must simply dissolve the blanket of identification with which you associate yourself. **You must let go of all the identities you give yourself.** You must realize that these identities have nothing to do with your true self. Your identity is temporary. YOU are eternal.

Once you dissolve the temporary identifications that you confuse for yourself, what is left will be your permanent core, your limitless soul—YOU. You will realize that your ego's need to identify itself was blinding you for illusory closure. You will realize that you were never lost. You must always look within for permanent results. Looking externally will always lead you to a temporary and illusory sense of self. Looking externally for your sense of self would be no different from identifying your head or your hand as your true self. You are not a physical being. You have just taken physical form. You are boundless. You are limitless. You are Light.

The Answers Are Within You

Let's imagine the entire universe as a basic building with ten floors. This building has no elevators and windows. The only way to get to the top is by using the stairs. You must walk through each floor to get to the next. Now I want you to imagine yourself walking into the lobby of the building. This is the first floor. Explore the first floor. Now take the stairs to the second floor. Do the same as you did on the first floor. Explore. Discover. See what the second floor has to offer. Now walk back to the stairs and up to the third floor. Walk around. Look at the entire space of the third floor. Pay attention to the paint on the walls, the tiles on the floor, the doors separating each room, and the placement of the furniture. Now go back to the staircase to walk up to the fourth floor. Walk up the stairs and open the door. Wait. There's a problem. The door is locked, and guess what? You don't have the key! Well, you are now limited to the third floor. You know what the second and first floors have to offer. You know this because to get to the third floor, you had to walk through each floor below it. However, you don't know what the fourth, fifth, sixth, seventh, eighth, ninth, and tenth floors look like. So, you come to understand that there is no way of getting to the fourth floor and beyond through the door by the staircase, so you try alternatives. You go back down to the first floor and exit the building. You use a ladder to try to see what is on the fourth floor only to realize that the building is windowless. You try to scale the building and break through the wall of the fourth floor only to realize that it is reinforced with steel. Physically, you have no way to enter. So, you do the only thing you can to try to understand what the fourth floor and beyond looks like. You use what is on the first floor, the second floor, and the third floor to theorize how the remaining floors look like.

This is exactly what is going on in the world today. Billions of dollars are spent every year trying to get farther into space and deeper into the ocean. We are constantly trying to figure out what exists on the fourth floor through the means of the first, second, and third floors. **We've become experts of**

the physical world around us but know little to nothing about the spiritual world within us. The fourth floor and beyond is the spiritual world within us. **Trying to understand the spiritual realm through physical means is not possible.** The physical cannot measure the spiritual, let alone understand it. **The key to the fourth floor and every floor above the fourth floor is introspection.** Introspection is the practicing of *diving within*. It is the key to elevation—the key that will grant you access to every floor above the third floor, the key that will allow you to access the infinite realm of the formless.

A Portal to Infinity

Introspection is a portal to the formless, where no limitation exists. It is the gateway that bridges the physical with the spiritual. To introspect is to dive within, to connect to your soul, and to connect to the universe on all levels of being and understanding. Introspection is the practice of observing yourself without the limitations of your mind but with the limitless nature of your soul. **There is no understanding. There is just feeling.** Introspection connects you to the place of stillness within you, where your true soul resides. Indulge in new experiences. Pay attention to your surroundings. Spend time alone. Write. Meditate. These are all practices that will open the doors to introspection. **The more you practice, the more floors you will explore.** You will no longer be stuck to just the third floor of physical experience. You will gain access to the portal to infinity.

Although you experience physical life through the lens of the third floor, your essence exists on every floor. Just because you experience your physical life on the third floor does not mean you are stuck to just the third floor and below. **Physicality is not your limitation.** This is just an illusion. On the contrary, the physical dimension of life is just a little fraction of the infinite spiritual realm, the formless realm. Your soul exists in every dimension. Therefore, you have access to every dimension of being. Since these higher dimensions are spiritually oriented, there is no physical entrance. You will never find a physical key because there is no door to unlock outside of yourself. No matter how advanced technology becomes, as long as the technology is physically oriented, true access to the formless realm will never be reached. **A physical key does not exist.** No physical scientific tools will allow us to transcend to different dimensions. These tools will only give us the illusion that we are advancing when, in reality, we are only discovering more of what we do not know and cannot know through the physical realm. These tools will only allow us to further dissect and explore the third floor and thus further theorize about what exists on the floors above.

The key is introspection. **Since your essence exists in every dimension, every dimension also exists within you.** To gain access to the infinite and formless realm, you must dive within. After all, the answer to a question such as "What is the formless realm?" is not something you can answer or understand with external means, such as language. The answer to such a question is an internal experience, a feeling, **an intuitive understanding**. Introspection is the portal to the formless realm, and intuition is your guide through the formless realm. Both introspection and intuition bring you closer to the meditative state that will enable you to access the oneness and eternal nature of the universe.

Accessing Intuition

The fourth floor is where the mind ends and the spirit begins. To gain access to the fourth floor and beyond, you must let go of the mind and embrace the spirit. To access these levels of the universe is to enter the intuitive realm. You must let intuition be your guide, as it is the only guide that can navigate the intuitive realm. Intuition, in its most basic form, is the ability to feel energy and act on the feeling without needing to reason or rationalize. Once you allow intuition to become your guide, blinded reason that is constrained with the limitations of the mind will disappear. To practice introspection effectively and transcend beyond the physical limitation of your body, you must learn to listen to the intuitive nature of your soul. **To further connect with your intuition, you must reconnect with your instinct.** Instinct is the reason a zebra stays away from a lion and why a bird flies away from a cat. Instinct is what leads a woman to nurse her child. **The more in touch you are with your instincts, the more apparent your intuition will become to you.** Intuition is simply further evolved instinct.

To access the realm of intuition, you must practice perceiving the universe through the language of energy. The law of cause and effect, the law of conservation, vibration and frequency, and the language of color—these concepts are the basis of the language of energy. **If you begin to think in terms of energy, frequency, and vibration, then intuition will become your natural leader and guide throughout your life.** Letting intuition guide you will get you much further than letting reason guide you. Intuition will bring you further, and it does so faster. Being in touch with instinct will bring you closer to intuition.

For years, there has been debate over whether meat is meant for human consumption, and for just as long, people have been trying to prove both sides of the argument. Instinct can solve this debate in a matter of seconds. Instinct will show you the answer based on truth instead of opinion, which is intuition over reason. Consider a hungry human baby. Put an apple and a rabbit in front of that baby. The baby will play with the rabbit and eat the apple. Alternatively, take a hungry baby lion. Put an apple and a rabbit in front of it. The lion will play with the apple and eat the rabbit.

Within instinct exists no falsity. It is the universe acting through you. This is intuition. Intuition stems from the core of the energetic universe, which is truth. There is no falsity or limitation within intuition. All reason exists within the intuitive realm. To connect to the realm of intuition is to acquire immediate reason. Reason can and should be used for practical and logical purposes. However, you must remember that to prevent being blinded by reason, you must always let intuition be a part of your guidance through the realm of reason. **To connect to the realm of intuition is to use a calculator over a pen and paper to solve a difficult equation.** It is efficient, it is powerful, and most importantly, it is the truth. To be in touch with intuition is to be in touch with your instinct and the interconnectivity of the universe. The intuition I am referring to is to be used for the purposes of elevating your soul. That is where it will guide you best. Intuition is a portal to the formless realm—an accessible portal. **Practice listening to intuition, and eventually, your intuition will become your instinct.** Connect to it. Listen to it. Trust it!

The Power of Meditation

Many confuse meditation for *thinking about nothing*. It's time to reshape that view. Meditation is an extremely powerful and accessible tool to use for introspection. You do not have to sit cross-legged on top of a mountain in Tibet. You do not have to dress like a monk. **Meditation is simply the practice of being present.** It is not an action. It is a state of mind. Whether you are in solitude on a mountaintop or drinking coffee on the subway on your way to work, it makes no difference. You must induce yourself into a state of presence at all times. This means you should be aware. This means you should be conscious of your surroundings. This means you should be here and now. You must pay attention to every breath, every thought, and every action. Not as something you are doing, but rather something that is just happening. This is meditation.

To attain this level of presence, you must constantly and consistently practice inducing yourself into an aware state of mind. Make it a habit to ask yourself if you are present and aware every hour you are awake to keep yourself in check. When first starting to apply this, you will find that your mind generally drifts off into the illusory past and future. This is okay. **Have no judgment. Simply bring your attention back to the present moment.** Pay attention to every breath. Become aware of every thought. Dissolve your unconscious patterns with consciousness. Shed Light on any darkness that you discover within you. As you practice presence, you will start to see that your predominant state of mind will naturally start shifting into one of presence. You will naturally be more connected to the formless realm. Your intuitive nature will start to become more and more apparent. As this occurs, you will start to see the world around

you differently. The way you think and, therefore, the way you feel will drastically improve.
You will gain a much higher degree of control
in every aspect of your life. What will start as a
predominant meditative state will evolve into
the desire to dive deeper.

Practicing Meditation

So, how do you actually access the power
of meditation? **Practice.** The easiest way to
get into a pure state of meditation is through
the use of sound. You must begin by listening.
Simply listen to each and every sound that
exists around you. **Don't identify what each
sound is**, rather just hear each sound for the
noise that it is creating. More importantly,
don't judge the sounds. Whether it be the
wind, a traffic jam, a sneeze, or the morning
birds, just listen. Don't let any sound bother
or frustrate you. **Just listen to each for what
they are.** Next time you listen to someone

speaking, practice listening to each word. Don't make sense of the words; just listen to the sounds that each one creates.

Thoughts are just internal sounds. Nevertheless, they are sounds. As you hear these thoughts in your mind, simply listen to them just as you would listen to sounds in the world around you. You must listen to them just as you listen to the wind, a traffic jam, or a sneeze. Look at your own thoughts as nothing but noises, and you will come to realize that **your internal experience and external experience are one**. Your thoughts are no different from the traffic jam, the wind, and the sneeze. They are all sounds. All you are doing is listening to them.

As you start your meditation, allow your breath to continue as it usually does. Let your breath flow in the way it would like to with no intentional breathing exercises. **You will come to realize that your breath is**

both a voluntary and involuntary action. On the one hand, you can voluntarily choose to breathe in a certain way. On the other hand, if you choose not to focus your attention on your breath, you will continue breathing involuntarily. In other words, the breathing will be happening to you. For this reason, **breath is the most important part of meditation**. Breath shows us that the division between what we voluntarily do and what involuntarily happens to us is an illusion. **Both the voluntary and involuntary aspects of your experience of life are all one.**

So, is life happening to you, or are you making life happen? On the one hand, the sun rises, and the sun sets. Temperature varies from cold to hot. Through this perspective, life happens to you just as breathing occurs when you are asleep. However, there exists another perspective where you are making life happen just as breathing occurs during voluntary and mindful breathing exercises. As the famous philosopher Alan Watts once said, "Your eyes turn the sun into light. Your nerve endings turn vibrations in the air into heat and temperature. Your eardrums turn vibrations in the air into sound." You are creating your world. The truth is, both of these perspectives are true. **You are just as much the doer as you are the experiencer.**

Listen to your own internal feeling and thoughts as if they were sounds, not something you are doing but just something that is happening. **Watch your breath as a happening that is not voluntary or involuntary, rather just as something that is occurring.** Simply become aware of these sensations. Don't hurry. Don't worry. Just be content that you are aware of what is going on in the present moment. This is meditation. As you practice this meditation through the medium of sound, you will come to realize that silence is where it all emerges from.

The Sound of Silence

Solitude was the consistent theme that connected all my injuries. Throughout my times of recovery, silence was my best friend. Naturally, the time I was forced to spend with myself led me into deep and intense journeys of self-reflection and meditation. Since I did not have the distraction of family and friends on a constant basis, I naturally paid attention to different things.

One morning when I was recovering from my infection in the hospital, I woke up to complete silence. The only thing I could hear was my heartbeat. I listened intensely for about ten minutes. There was one thing that I just couldn't get past: **the moment of silence in between each beat**. So, I tried imagining my heartbeat without the moment of silence in between, and I immediately realized that **without the silence, there would be no beat**. I understood that the moment of silence in between each beat is what makes it possible for the heart to beat in the first place. This experience led me to the realization of how important silence is. What would music be without the silence between each beat? What would language be without the silence between each word? **Silence is what gives the ability for anything to exist.**

As you dive deeper, you will start to realize and become aware of many things around you and within you. One of the most important foundations you will come to realize is that solitude and silence are where all growth occurs. The heart would not beat without the silence between each beat, and that moment of silence is the expression of the formless realm. It is what creates anything and everything. The practice of paying attention to this silence and spending time with yourself will be the largest catalyst to your growth as a spiritual being.

Whether in isolation or silence, you are never alone. However, you are never with anybody else either. **You are always with yourself.** Even when you are in a room with one hundred people, you will always experience your own reality by yourself, and everyone you are *with* will experience their own reality of the same moment with themselves. Although you may be enjoying your experiences with other people throughout your life, it is important to understand that **you are always experiencing the present moment with yourself**. This realization changes the feeling of being alone. You come to understand that whether you are surrounded by one hundred people or surrounded by no one, it makes no difference. You are always with the only person you can truly be with—YOU.

PART TWO

Illusions

The physical dimension through which we experience life is filled with illusion. Dissolve the illusions, and only then will you be able to live a life of limitless potential.

CHAPTER 7

Separation

**Separation is an
illusion because all
cannot be divided
into separate parts. All
contains everything; it
leaves nothing out.**
—Michael Jeffreys

The grand illusion we refer to as *separation* is beyond what any illusionist or magician can fathom. Since all form stems from the formless, the only differentiation between one form and another is the combination of form the formless takes. **All form stems from the formless.** Everything and everybody is an expression of the formless. Separation cannot exist. It is an illusion that we live by.

The formless realm is the very proof of this. It deems all of existence as one limitless realm of possibility.

The illusion of separation only exists because of the egos need to feel whole and in control. This false need has led humanity to be guided by illusion. This illusion will lead to the fall of humanity if not dissolved. The reality here is that **we live in a universe that is built on interdependent systems.** Nothing can exist independent of anything else. **Everything that exists only exists relative to everything else.**

To better understand this concept, envision two sticks leaning against each other. Each stick is only standing because the other is pushing against it. If one stick is removed, the other will fall. They are interdependent. The universe and everything in it work no differently. **The universe is one infinite realm of interdependent systems.** We, along with our environments, are interdependent. We are all interdependent. We only exist physically in relation to the space around us. We only know who we are in terms of other people. These systems cannot be separated from one another. No systems can be separated from one another. This includes both your internal and external environments. **The illusion of separating the inseparable has led our society onto a profoundly sick path.** What you call the external world is as much you as your own body. As a famous Sufi master once said, **"You are not a drop in the ocean. You are the entire ocean in a single drop."** The problem is that we have not been taught to think and feel this way. The myths underlying culture and common sense have not taught us to feel identical with the universe. The truth is **each and every one of us IS the eternal universe.**

Separating the Inseparable

We live in a society that is built on the illusion of separation. We have all been taught by society to see and think through this illusion. We have become used to dividing life into pieces. Our lives are built on separation. As infants, we didn't identify with anything. However, over time, we identified with our names and our bodies. We started believing that our names and bodies were what separated us from the rest of the world. We believed that our names and bodies defined us. We alienated ourselves from the rest of the universe along with every person we meet.

What happens, in turn, is the need and desire to reconnect to what we believe that we have separated from—the inseparable universe, the formless realm. We seek close and intimate relationships with others to gain this feeling of interconnectedness and wholeness once again. The problem is that we believe that we are limited to our physical body. We see it as the boundary that separates us from the rest of the world. We think we are our body. We identify with our body. So, as we try to get closer to the formless realm, we always keep our distance because getting too close will threaten the identity we have created for ourselves. It will threaten the ego.

We Are Blind

Once upon a time, six blind men who lived in a town in India thought they were very clever. Every day, they argued with each other about who was smarter. One day, an elephant came into town. The men had never heard of an elephant, so they all decided to go and experience the elephant. They could not see it, but they could smell it, hear it, and feel it. Each man touched a different part of the elephant to experience just what it was.

The first man touched the elephant's body. He concluded that an elephant is like a wall. The second man touched one of the elephant's tusks. He concluded that it is not like a wall, but it is more like a spear. The third man touched the elephant's trunk. He concluded that the elephant is not like a wall or a spear but more like a snake. The fourth man touched one of the elephant's legs. He concluded that an elephant is not like a wall, a spear, or a snake but more like a big tree trunk. The fifth man touched one of the elephant's ears. He concluded that an elephant is not like a wall, a spear, a snake, or a tree but like a fan. The sixth man touched the elephant's tail. He concluded that all the other men were wrong because an elephant is like a rope. A little boy who could actually see the elephant heard the blind men arguing and told them that they were all wrong, since not one of them felt the entire elephant. This story is a direct reflection of our world today.

We live in a world of blind men. Up until about one hundred years ago, it was common to find one person who was an expert in multiple fields. Those days have passed. One man studied astrology, astronomy, mathematics, and biology and was, therefore, able to realize all the connections between them. Then, a big change occurred. Experts in specific fields started emerging. The educational system led students to choose one field of interest and become an expert in a specific aspect of that field. This has led us on an intense path of technological progression; however, it is all at the cost of illusory separation. **We are lacking the ability to make bridges and connections between all fields of study because we see each field as separate from the other.** This illusion of separation keeps us blind to the interconnectivity of the universe.

Living by the illusion of separation has led our society to become mentally and physically sick. It is responsible for racism. It is responsible for crime. It is responsible for sickness. Society has led its members to become specialized with no regard to interconnectivity. This is not to suggest that specialization is a negative thing. On the contrary, it has led our society to progress immensely. However, **specialization with no regard to the interconnectivity of the universe is useless**. An expert in one field without the understanding that all fields of study are connected is no different from a blind man touching only one part of the elephant. You may become an expert of its tail; however, you will never see what a true elephant looks like unless you understand that there is no separation between the tail and the body. The tail cannot exist separate from the elephant. It only exists in relation to its body.

Our habit of separating the inseparable has led us to a sick place. The doctor is the expert in prescribing drugs while the scientist is the expert in creating those drugs. **The practice and the research are divided.** We have divided the indivisible. **We have separated the inseparable.** The moment our society became overrun by the illusion of separation, the bridges connecting all disciplines became invisible to the mind, and the interconnectivity of the universe was forgotten. The illusion of separation overtook us all. We are taught to see physics as separate from biology and astronomy as separate from psychology. We are taught to see the heart as separate from the stomach and the mind as separate from the body. All these systems are interdependent on one another. They exist only in relation to each other. They cannot be separated.

Creating Sickness

Conventional science is based on a reductionist point of view of the world. In other words, it takes the universe apart and studies it in pieces. It is based on the illusion that separation exists. This will only lead to an illusory conclusion, since each piece of the universe is interdependent on the next. To study each piece of the universe as separate from the next without understanding that each piece is necessary to create the big picture is to study falsity.

Letting the illusion of separation guide us has led us all to live in a physically sick society. It has led our doctors to focus on the physical realm instead of the energetic realm. It has led our doctors to only examine the body of a sick patient without giving attention to everything else that affects the body, such as its environment, family, job, and so on. **To study illness, you must dissolve the**

illusion of separation. You must study holistically. This means to study with the knowledge of the whole picture instead of breaking it up to separate pieces. Illusory separation is the reason it is difficult for doctors to understand why nutrition plays a role in health. Doctors are taught to see the heart as separate from the liver and the lungs as separate from the kidneys. Our organs are all interconnected. **What affects one part of our body will indeed affect the rest.** This is because we are one body made up of interdependent systems. We are no different from the universe. **We are identical to the universe.** We ARE the universe.

The illusion of separation stems from the fact that we have not been taught to think and feel as though we are identical with the universe. This lack of understanding has led us to see everything in the universe as separate from one another. This illusion has shaped the way our society operates. The lack of understanding of the interconnectivity of the universe results from the illusion of separation. **The universe is an infinite number of interdependent systems that work together to create one limitless entity just as your body is made up of interdependent systems that create YOU.**

The Terminology Crisis

The illusion of separation has created the deceptive divide between the words and the stories we use to describe anything and everything. With the help of our egos, humanity has succeeded in creating so many different words and stories to get the same message across.

The ego is so caught up with the terminology used to get a message across that we completely forget the message and let our ego separate us instead of letting the formless unify us. Whether we are talking about religion or the creation of the universe, how it happened is irrelevant. The stories associated with each are simply used to explain an idea, a belief, or a principle. Identifying with these stories creates the illusory separation between all ideas.

In the case of the creation of the universe, whether you are a devout Christian who believes that "God created the universe in six days and rested on the seventh" or an atheist who believes that it was the big bang, it makes no difference. Both agree that the universe was created. However, the attachment each side has to their unknown story line of events with which they have identified is the root of their disagreement. The identification with one story line over another is what creates separation instead of unification. So next time you disagree with somebody about a belief you have identified with, don't be defensive. Simply let go of your identification and break down each belief to its core. You will realize that the disagreement lies within your identification with a story, not the idea. The only difference is within the stories being used to describe the same idea. Once you dissolve identification with the story that has been created to spread a message, disagreement will be a pastime, and the ego will live no more.

CHAPTER 8

Time

**I have realized that the
past and the future are real
illusions, that they exist in
the present, which is what
there is and all there is.**

—Alan Watts

When thinking about the idea of time, most of us tend to think in terms of beginning and end or birth and death because of the ego's need to separate the inseparable. We believe that time moves in a one-way flow from the past, to the present, and into the future. We believe that what happens now and what will happen in the future are always a result of what happened in the past. This is an illusion. Time is an illusion.

We have been taught that time is something real. We have been taught that we live along some intangible and invisible timeline between birth and death. Most of all, we have been taught that we must spend this time wisely or we are *wasting our time*. Time was created by human beings. The clock, the calendar—these are all imperfect tools that were created to indicate our positions relative to other things as well as other people. It can be very helpful for practical purposes, such as allowing us to arrange events, make a train, schedule meetings, celebrate birthdays, and so on. The problem is that we have become slaves to it. We have forgotten its true cause of creation and now live by the illusion that it actually exists. Its misconception has turned the tables, and it now controls us. Once you understand the illusion of time, you will be able to use it instead of letting it use you. You will no longer be stuck in the past or worried about the future. You will live in the only place that truly exists—the NOW.

Now

The past does not exist, and neither does the future. Anything that ever happened in the past happened in the present moment at the time that it occurred. Anything that will happen in the future will happen in the present moment when it does happen. **All past moments happened in the present moment, and all future moments will happen in the present moment.** Think back to an important time in your life. For the sake of an example, let's refer back to the day you were born. When you were born, it happened in the present moment. Your physical manifestation that you call your body was created in what is called a "NOW moment." **The NOW is where all existence arises from.** It is where all sound emerges from. It is where all events happen. **The NOW is the only moment that exists**, and once this concept is understood, the illusion of how we experience the passage of time will become apparent.

The Relative Reality

Albert Einstein revolutionized physics and astronomy after publishing his theory of special relativity in 1905. He challenged Sir Isaac Newton's accepted view that time is absolute and forward-moving and concluded that time is actually relative and can both stretch and contract. Moreover, Einstein concluded that time is relative to your position and speed on Earth and deduced that the faster you move through space, the slower you move through time. Einstein's theory of special relativity proves that time is indeed a relative reality and not a fundamental reality.

I want you to imagine a railroad track that wraps around the entire circumference of the Earth. **The train on the track wraps around the entire track, with no beginning or end.** You hop aboard the train in New York City and begin your journey around the world. There are twenty stops along the way, including cities, forests, islands, and oceans. The first stop after New York City is Los Angeles. You are currently on the train approaching the city; however, you are not quite there yet. In this moment, you perceive Los Angeles as being something you are going to see in the future. You finally arrive in Los Angeles and experience it in your present moment. After a few hours of touring the city, you board the train and continue on the journey. Los Angeles is now behind you. It is now in what you perceive as your past. The next stop is Hawaii. Once again, you perceive Hawaii in your future until you arrive on the magnificent island.

After you leave the island, it falls back into your past, and the cycle continues.

Before you arrived in both Los Angeles and Hawaii, did they exist? Of course! Once you reached each destination, did they exist? Of course! After you left each destination, did they exist? Of course! **You only perceive each destination in the future before you arrive and in the past, after you leave based on your physical position on the train track relative to each destination.** However, the fact is, no matter what your position is on the train track, **all train stops exist simultaneously** whether it is in what you perceive as your future or your past. In other words, New York City, Los Angeles, and Hawaii all exist in the same moment although they are in different time zones. The only reason they are in your past, present, or future is because of your physical location in relation to them. This is relativity. **Time is relative.** It is not a fundamental truth of the universe; rather, **it is simply an illusion as a result of how our conscious experience is situated.**

The train on the track is a direct reflection of how we experience the passage of time as human beings it also shows us why our experience is simply an illusion. As previously stated, the train has twenty stops around the world. **Each destination exists simultaneously with every other destination**; however, we experience each destination in our timeline of past, present, and future based on our physical location on the train track.

We perceive our lives through the linear and forward-moving passage of time for **two simple reasons**. The first reason is **we experience the train track from one fixed point as the passenger**, and the second reason is **there are multiple stops on the track which act as points of reference to travel between**. However, if you could leave your body and view the entire track from space, your experience would no longer be from one physical point on the track, and the **entire experience would be happening simultaneously**. You would quickly understand that what you previously identified as past, present, and future based on your physical location relative to an identified point is all happening in the same moment—the NOW.

Have you ever tried looking at one point in space in front of a moving object? If you haven't, give it a try. Whether it is flowing water or a moving train, try to stare at one point in space with the flowing water or moving train in the background. You will surely experience difficulty. Your eyes will rapidly move from side to side. Why? Because we are hardwired to always look at one fixed point. It is simply the way the universe has created us.

Your conscious experience is built in just the same way. It is situated like that of a passenger on the train. **Your conscious experience is situated as one fixed point in the eternal cycle of the universe through which we experience our physical reality.**

Within this eternal cycle of the universe is all existence in one single moment, with no separate points to travel between. Time can only be perceived if there are points of reference to travel between. Identifying a beginning and an end of anything creates these illusory points of reference and, therefore, feeds the illusion of time. Why illusory? Because by identifying points of reference, you are separating oneness, which is inherently inseparable, and what is separation? An illusion! It is important to remember that these points of reference are not universal truths; rather, they are realities created by us to make the inconceivable and inseparable oneness of the universe more comprehensible.

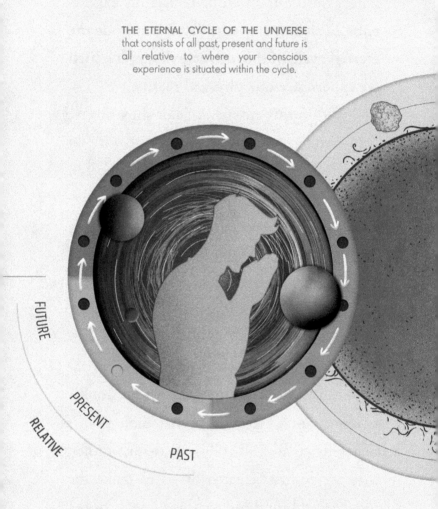

THE ETERNAL CYCLE OF THE UNIVERSE that consists of all past, present and future is all relative to where your conscious experience is situated within the cycle.

FUTURE

PRESENT

RELATIVE

PAST

YOUR CONSCIOUS EXPERIENCE
from the fixed point

SEPARATE EVENTS
created by definition

View from outside of the eternal cycle without the illusion of your fixed point conscious experience and without separate events.

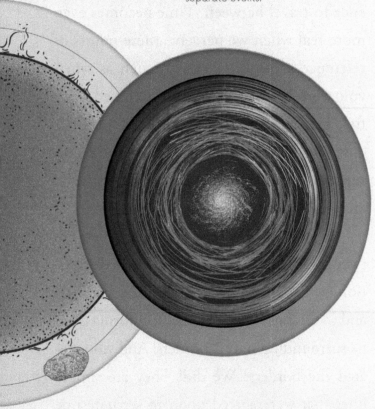

What was once experienced as past, present and future is now happening in one simultaneous moment... **THE NOW.**

The Grand Fallacy

Time only becomes real when we perceive there to be separate points of reference to travel between. Time becomes even more real when we perceive these points of reference as physical events, such as when you were born, when you purchased your first car, the day you got married, and the day you die, to name a few. **There are no separate events.** The question that must be answered first is "What is an event?"

Let's go back to the train track. There are twenty different destinations. Each destination is in a different state, a different country, and so on, but what separates California from its surrounding states? Borders! And who created the borders? We did! They are simply lines that were agreed upon to separate one state from another. The truth is, there is no true separation between California and New York other than that which we created. They are part of the same land. They are one. This book poses as another example. Where does it begin? The front cover? The introduction? The acknowledgments? Chapter one? All these are valid beginning points; however, it is our agreed-upon definition that creates what we call the *beginning*. This leads to an endless cycle that teaches us that **both beginning and end is based on what we collectively agree is the definition of a beginning and end**. We must always remember that we created these definitions. They are not real. **When something begins or ends is all a matter of definition.** Our agreement upon each definition is what gives each beginning and end validity. The fact is **there is no beginning, and there is no end.** Therefore, **there are no points of reference for time to travel between**.

Cause and Effect

We have been taught to think that all events are caused by previous events. This is not a universal truth; rather, it is simply a relative truth. To think this way is to resort to the illusion of separation. You may be asking yourself at this point, *If cause and effect is an illusion, why was the law of cause and effect a foundation?* Relative truths can be very beneficial so long as they are not confused with universal truths. Once you know how an illusion is formulated, it is no longer an illusion. However, the second you confuse the illusion for reality, it no longer serves a beneficial purpose. The illusion of cause and effect helps us organize the one continuous event we call the universe in our minds from the fixed point through which we consciously experience physical reality. The illusion of cause and effect acts as a guide that helps us achieve the goals we set for ourselves. However, we must always remember that it is something that we created for practical purposes. It is merely a tool just like time. It is not a truth of the universe.

Let's Be Practical

Although there are no separate events, **separating events simply for practical purposes is okay**. The practical separation of events is what allows us to write our history textbooks and teach about events that have occurred in order to learn from them. However, one must always remember that this separation is being done for practical purposes. Otherwise, you will get lost in the illusion once again and end up living a life of illusion.

For practical purposes, **we have divided all events that occur into smaller parts**. We did so by giving each identified event a beginning and an end. We did this for the sake of history and memory. For example, World War II began in 1939 and ended in 1945.

However, what led up to the war started way before 1939, and the consequences of the war lasted way past 1945. The dates of the war were identified for practical purposes; however, **the problem is that we forget that we did this, and we end up identifying the war as a separate event from all other events**. We now believe that events are separate from one another. This belief has created separate points of reference and, thus, leads us to the illusion of the linear and forward-moving passage of time. It leads us to believe that the present is a result of the past when, indeed, the **past is a result of the present.**

You might ask, *"How can time be an illusion if I remember yesterday?"* This is a valid question with a simple answer. Now is all that exists. Now encompasses all past, present, and future in one continuous and ever-present moment. You simply experienced yesterday as a different day because you, as a human being, experience reality from a fixed point within the eternal cycle of the universe. So, from this fixed point of experience, of course, time exists. However, it is simply a relative reality and not a fundamental truth. In other words, it's an illusion and not a foundation. It is always important to remember that if we were to zoom out of the fixed point by which we experience our reality, we would see the eternal cycle of the universe where all past, present, and future exist simultaneously in one moment—the NOW.

The Illusion of Memory

Memory provides us with the ability to perceive time as a linear and forward moving passage. It creates the illusion that time flows from the past, to the present and into the future. The truth is, if there was no memory, there would be no time. Our memory of the past tells us what we have done, and we therefore define who we are through it. You may need factual memory for practical purposes such as remembering your name, but this is not what we use memory for anymore. Many of us use memory to recollect what we see as events that happened in the past. When these events are perceived as negative events, this is where major damage and stagnation occurs. Doing so holds you to the past, in this case an unproductive and self-destructive past. If you insist on defining yourself by your past, that is your choice but this is an illusion. The fact is that it all starts now. Let go of the poisonous habit of thought where you define yourself as a result of what you've done. Instead, **adapt the healthier habit of thought where you define yourself based on what you are doing now.** Afterall, right now is the only time that exists. Doing so will liberate you from the illusion of time and unproductive memory. This is true freedom.

CHAPTER 9

Death

**Death is not the opposite
of life, but a part of it.**

—Haruki Murakami

Throughout my childhood, spending time outside was one of my favorite things to do. There was one tree in my backyard that I absolutely loved. It was my favorite tree. I felt a strong connection to it. One day, there was a terrible storm, and it ripped the tree right out of the ground. I was sad. I thought to myself, *"The tree is dead!"* Over the next few months, I visited that tree quite often, and what I saw was incredible. The tree started decomposing. After a few more months, I saw something even more incredible. Where the tree was decomposing, new life-forms were emerging.

I realized that it was **decomposing in order to recompose**. I realized the *death* of the tree I loved so much gave room for new life to come about. Fungus was growing. Bushes were emerging. Grass was flourishing. The only question I could ask myself was, "How can life come out of death?" My conclusion was very simple. It cannot.

We have been taught that to die is a terrible thing. This poisonous way of thinking has been instilled within us by our society. This is because our society is run by the ego. Have you ever thought about the idea of death without the fear that society has instilled within you? Have you ever asked yourself what it would be like to go to sleep and never wake up? Well, **what was it like to wake up after having never gone to sleep?** After all, you have experienced this. We all have. This is what happened when you were born.

The Concept of Death

Death is an interesting concept, an interesting word, and an interesting idea. Above all, **death is an illusion. If life exists now, life must have always existed in one form or another.** In no-life, which is the absence of life, ever existed, then life would never be able to come out of no-life. It is this realization that bridges the illusory gap between life and death. There is no gap. They are merely two phases of the same cycle—the cycle of life. The only thing that exists is life. Death is just a concept that we assigned to a part of the cycle of life to make it more comprehensible. This is your ego speaking.

The word for *death* translates very differently based on what language you speak. The word *death* in English refers to an end. However, the word for death in the ancient language of Sufi, a mystical branch of Islam that seeks the annihilation of the ego, directly translates to *westing*. Why? Because they saw that the sun rises in the east and sets in the west. They understood that just as the sun comes up, the sun goes down, and the next day, it comes right back up again, and the cycle continues. They intuitively understood that **death is just another part of the cycle of life**. They intuitively understood the principles behind the law of conservation.

The law of conservation proves that death is an illusion. As you know, **energy cannot be created or destroyed. The only thing energy can do is transform.** So, where did the fungus, the bushes, and the grass emerge from as the tree was decomposing? The tree! All these new life-forms emerged from the energy of the tree. The only difference between the tree, the fungus, the bush, and the grass are the combinations of formless energy that each new form takes. In other words, the way the decomposed matter recomposes. This is the cycle of life.

Death cannot exist in the cycle of life. Only transformation may exist in the cycle of life. To the human mind, the transformation of one form into another form may seem like death, but this is just an illusion. If new life can come out of decomposed matter, then that matter was never dead because life cannot arise from no-life. **Life can only arise from life.** Death is just a different part of the cycle of life. It is the energy of the tree that made it possible for that new fungus, bush, and grass to grow. This is not death. This is transformation.

Identity Dies

The question remains: What *died* when my favorite tree was ripped out of the ground? After all, the tree I loved so much was no longer there for me to sit under. The only thing that died was the identity of the tree—the identity that I gave it. "A tree," "my favorite tree." Identity is temporary. It is bound to birth and death. This is because what you are identifying is a physical form which is bound to change form. All physical form is temporary. Sooner or later, **when the form you assign an identity to transforms, that identity is no longer present, and you confuse this for death**. If we identify with our physical form, then we bind ourselves to the illusion of death. Although identification is temporary and bound to the limitations of the physical realm, energy (the soul) is eternal and exists according to the limitless nature of the formless realm. Your body is a temporary form. You are not your body. You are not your form. You are more than just what you do. You are more than just what you call yourself. **You are the awareness behind your thoughts.** You are the limitless and boundless energy that is the formless realm. You are everything and everyone. You are consciousness. **You are a soul.**

Wake Up

Most of us live a life of illusion. We are asleep. Wake up! You will know that you are awake when you no longer fear your own death. You will know that you are awake when you no longer mourn the death of a loved one. Once you understand that death is an illusion, there will no longer be something or somebody to mourn. On the contrary, there will only be something to celebrate. The day that death befalls you or your loved one is the day that the soul continues into the realm of free and formless expression. **It is the soul's transformation day!** Why would you be sad that you or somebody else is celebrating their transformation to spiritual freedom? We mourn out of selfishness, not out of love. To mourn out of love would be to celebrate the soul's transformation! You may mourn **your loss** of their physical expression;

however, mourning **their death** is to be sad about something that never happened.

This is not a new idea whatsoever. This idea has existed since the beginning of time and is a basic foundation in all major religions today. Every religion teaches us that death is merely an illusion. Every religion teaches us that the soul outlives the body and the mind. Wake up, and your outlook on death will be changed forever. It will no longer be something to fear. It will only be something to celebrate.

Transcending Death

Your body is the home in which your soul resides in. One day your physical body will have to change form. It will have to decompose in order to recompose. Your identity will be no more, but your soul will continue to manifest different forms and take on new identities. Let go of your ego's need to limit the limitless to feel whole. **Dissolve your attachment to the identification you give temporary form, and you will transcend the illusion of death.** It is this understanding that dissolves the fear of death. The second you understand what you fear is an illusion, there will no longer be anything to fear. You will be free of fear, free of limitation, and free of illusion. You will wake up. This is true freedom. **Letting go of the fear of death will become effortless the moment you realize that death happens to an identification, and not to YOU.**

Hopefully, by now, you understand that we live in a world of illusion. You understand that what you see is not always what it seems to be. You can now see through the process of domestication that society has instilled within us and break through it to live a life of limitless potential and possibilities. You are no longer bound to the ideas of beginning, end, birth, death, creation, destruction, good, and bad. These are now apparent illusory words to you. As long as the foundations are understood, you should now have gained an awareness and understanding of the basic building blocks of the universe and will be able to think in terms of energy, vibration, and frequency. Practice walking on this new path of thought, and the control you have over every aspect of your life will be limitless. You will attain a higher level of consciousness. You will be granted access to the formless realm, where all form is created, and thus become the creator of all creation that manifests into your life. Dissolve your ego, practice the language of energy, experiment with the line of manifestation, appreciate the harmony of balance, and dive within! Only then will you truly understand the illusions that are embedded in every corner of the universe.

I encourage you to reread every chapter multiple times and refer to this book periodically. Doing so will allow you to dive deeper and access more information and wisdom that is already within you. You must always remember that you are here for a purpose. Never let the physical realm blind you. It is an illusion that has the power to forever keep you hostage in the world of limitation, but this is not your purpose. This is not why you are here. You are simply a soul living in a temporary home that you call your body—a soul who has decided to come here to fulfill a purpose. Contrary to popular belief, you are not here to just eat, sleep, work, and reproduce. You are here for a greater purpose—a spiritual purpose. We all are. A new wave of consciousness is coming upon us. It has already started. More and more of us are becoming aware of who we truly are, and we are dissolving the false identities of who we once thought we were. We are powerful spiritual beings of energy. We have no limitations other than the ones we give reality to through our beliefs. Our thoughts are what manifest anything and everything into our lives. Think carefully, be calculated, and form your seeds of thought specifically to your preferences.

You now have access to valuable information that can and should be used for the greater good. Use it to open your doors of thought and bring it to a higher level than when you received it. We are each a piece of a puzzle who serves the purpose in fulfilling the whole picture. We are each equally important. Without each and every one of us, no matter how small or large the piece, the picture will never be whole. We are limitless spiritual beings who have the power to manifest anything that we desire. May you enjoy your journey of elevation and may you bring others along the way. May you shine Light where darkness now resides. May you dive within and access the limitless core of the universe. That which is one, whole, eternal, unchanging, limitless, and timeless—**the formless realm.**

You are the creator.

You are the soul.

You are the universe.

We are ONE.

So, what are you waiting for? Use your limitless power to spread consciousness across all of humanity and become a part of the new wave that is upon us. You will know you are ready when you no longer have to ask yourself if you are ready. Let us spread the Light together.

I wish you a journey filled with
Light, Peace, and Love.
L.P.L

Jason Shurka is a spiritual teacher who focuses on teaching others how to use their mind to clear all emotional and physical blockages in order to unlock their limitless potential. He takes pleasure in traveling the world and exploring different cultures. He has dedicated his life to shining the light of presence and love on others and thus expanding the Light for others to shine onto the rest of humanity. Jason currently lives in Long Island, New York.

CPSIA information can be obtained
at www.ICGtesting.com
Printed in the USA
LVHW021325080920
665327LV00003B/415

9 781646 285112